COME
CLIMB
MY
HILL

Words
    WINSTON O. ABBOTT
Drawings
    BETTE EATON BOSSEN

$$\overline{IHP}$$

Published By
INSPIRATION HOUSE
South Windsor, Connecticut

REVISED EDITION

Fourteenth Printing 1992

ISBN 0-918114-03-9

This book is a companion volume to

SING WITH THE WIND

HAVE YOU HEARD THE CRICKET SONG

COME WALK AMONG THE STARS

and

LETTERS FROM CHICKADEE HILL

because—
    you have listened
       to the heartbeat of the earth
    you are especially invited to —
                —
              —
                  —

come climb my hill
and share with me —
the quietude of woodland paths —
the friendly patter of the rain —
evening skies splashed with the
crimson fires of sunset —
vesper songs and wishing stars —
moon drenched meadows and the majesty of
storms —
come share these things of beauty—
come —
come climb my hill —

it was only a stalk of withered goldenrod —
                                but the
winter sun shone briefly and burnished it with
                                gold —
until the falling snow turned it into silver
                                crystal —
and I asked —
            is silver more beautiful than gold —
but there was no answer — yet somehow in the
silence I seemed to know that beauty has a
                        mood for every need —
    for strength the enduring purple hills —
                                        for
        courage the rugged oak upon a storm-
        swept ridge —
                for joy the songs of the birds at dawn
        and the peacefulness of sunlit meadows —
                                                —
                                                —
                                                —

and should your spirit need a promise of
    perfection —
                you may have the pink buds
of my mountain laurel —
                    and the fragile
snowflakes swirling eagerly toward the
familiar earth —
                and because life destines
that we share something of sadness —
together we will listen to the wood
    thrush
singing at the edge of dusk —
                        and in the
evening firelight — muse at the
    flickering
forms of unforgotten happiness —
                            and
                    sometimes pain —

it is the sense of mystery —
that gives to life —
its majesty —

for it comes — it goes —
                    it is the song of bird
upon the branch — it is the silence when the
song is gone —
                    it is as fragile as a spark before
the wind — and yet its light may rise to be
another star —
                    it is the radiance of the dawn —
and the mysterious pathway to the dark —
                                        and it
is not always easy to remember — that the
scattered embers of the afterglow —
                                        are banked by
some invisible hand —
                    to light the fires of
sunrise — in another day —

the frail spirit of man
has ever searched for —
and often found —
        strength
        in the shadows
        of the mountains —

for eyes lifted to the mountain are filled
with majesty and splendor —
                              the grey peak —
indistinct in the cold light of dawn — radiant
against the brightness of the noonday sun —
robed in soft purple as the twilight heralds
the approaching darkness — ethereal by the
wan light of the moon — and utterly lonely
through the misted curtain of the rain —
                                        but ever
a scene of splendor — and timeless as time itself
— for the changing seasons leave but a fleeting
mark upon the mountain —

                            —

                          —

                            —

—
—
—

some feathery green in early spring — pale
yellows and deeper greens — the golds and
crimsons of the fires of autumn —

                              but only
the snows of heaven reach above the
timberline — to add a crown of purity
where the mountain reaches upward to the
  sky —

              and the seasons pass —
              and pass again —
              but the mountain is
                         eternal —

for grandeur —
    for humility —
        reach up and touch
     the stars that shine upon my hill —

there is no defined boundary between the day-
light and the darkness — so deftly does twilight
blend the two with misted light and lengthening
shadows —
          perhaps the night begins when
the first star lights a taper in the deepening
dusk — or perhaps — when the dark canopy of
the sky is aglow with twinkling lights —
                                it does
not really matter — as long as we can reach a
hand upward into the heaven and stir the stars
about at will —
          humble at our insignificance in
the vast scheme of things — grateful that the
Creator has endowed our souls with wonder and
with awe —
          that we might better appreciate the
grandeur of a star-filled night —
                       and —
                            —
                               —
                                 —

—
—
—

    if we linger —
               as I have often done —
                         we will
see the slender fingers of the dawn — stealing
across the sleeping world — extinguishing one
by one the lanterns of the night —
                     and we will
share the sadness that touches the heart as the
darkness follows the light —
                 and also share the
joy that comes with the dawn — as the light
follows upon the darkness —

for courage —
          come and stand beneath
          my rugged oak —

it does take courage —

> even for an oak — to leave the sheltered
> forest — and stand alone upon a windswept
> ridge — where the storms sweep fiercely
> from the dark and ominous skies — and the
> winds scream shrilly with the icy voice of
> winter —

it does take courage —

> and strongly anchored roots — deep in the
> sustaining earth —

it does take courage —

> pure and primitive — to stand in a place
> of no retreat — to watch the lightning sear
> the sky — to feel the roll of thunder shake
> the earth — to face the elements — un-
> bowed and unafraid —

> > and yet —

> > —

> > —

—
—
—
there are days of calm and peace
and nights of sustaining strength —
when the wind rustles through the
trembling leaves and whispers —
what are
such trivial
things as scars —
to one
who shares the
night with stars —

only a Master Artist —
            can create a meadow —

framed   by weathered   posts   and   rambling
walls —

      that man might have some part in the
creation of the beautiful —

                and one day come to
know — that his spirit is enriched and strength-
ened in a place of serenity and peace —

                 a meadow —

                    where
the early morning mists first rise and linger
— where the grasses quietly sleep in the noonday sun — where only the gentlest of breezes
come to stir them from their dreaming — where
cool green shadows from the trees along the
hedgerow mark the day as past —

                 a meadow —

                    truly
a place of loveliness —

           made ever lovelier by the
tiny lights of fireflies moving through the scented
dusk —

softly —
    ever so softly —
    silently —
        ever so silently —
    from the
    sodden sky —

drifts the snow — hushing our busy world with
its mantle of whitened silence —

                              each flake swirls
eagerly from the sky — aware of its tiny impor-
tance — in covering the cold and waiting earth
—with a soft blanket of glistening white —

                                       even
the stalks of the lowliest weeds are clothed in
stately ermine — and stark branches are muted
into greater loveliness —

                           as the snow bestows its
beauty upon all who will receive it —

                                      —

                                        —

                                          —

—
—
—

deftly and gently each nook and crevice
is moulded into a garment for the earth —
angles and hummocks are blended into
gracious symmetry —
                and all traces of dross
and ugliness are quickly banished from our
sight —
        as the sodden sky —
            transforms its burden
            into beauty —

walk softly through this quiet wood
　　for here our dreams lie sleeping —
　　　　watched over by the friendly stars
　　　　and mourned by night winds weeping —

until the brightness of the dawn
　　shall bring a new to-morrow —
　　　　and love shall heal all aching hearts
　　　　and leave no room for sorrow —

sometime — somewhere —

upon an old wood road steeped in the autumn twilight — or upon a lonely beach where wisps of fog steal inland from the sea — or in a summer meadow where the moonlight pales the dark —

you may come upon the spirit of a dream — indistinct — elusive —

but you will know it is a part of you — for the heart remembers —

the crystal blue of shining waters before the grayness of the clouds — the beckoning stars before a night of raging storm — the fragrance of a rosebud before the petals scatter to the ground —

for the fabric of our life is woven — of both golden threads and dark —

and the gold will never tarnish — while the heart remembers —

my life —
            has been enriched —
                        and blessed —
by many unseen things —
            as fragile as —
            the frost
            upon a
            winter window —

where in the morning light appeared an artistry
of leaf and fern —
  etched upon the glass in powder gray and
  icy blue —
    a mystery from the darkness of
    the night —
        and so I came to know with childish
wisdom — that unseen power fills the world
about me —
    it mattered not — that mid-day sun erased
    this thing of beauty —

            for I had seen it
    long enough to know that it was real —
                as real
as — unseen things that give to life direction —
and lift it upward in its dark and troubled
hours —
            with faith — unseen —
            and love — unspoken —

the sea has many moods —
and mystery —

eternally restless is the sea —
                              with its ceaseless
flow and ebb of tides —
                              moving ever moving —
watched over by the graceful gulls — hovering
on tireless wings —
                              circling on the unseen wind —
    moving ever moving —
                              how eternally restless
is my spirit too —
                    how like the sea — with mo-
ments of exhilaration and moments of despair
—
    —
        —
            —

searching ever searching — for an answer
to life's flowing — ebbing tide —
                    if I were a gull
                    above the surging waters —
                    could I see
                    beyond the far horizon —
                    would I know
                    the answer —

there is something of magic
in the firelight —
and memories that come and go
amid the flickering shadows —

do you not know —
                    that cares and weariness and
unforgotten pain — drift upward with the curl-
ing smoke —
              and haunting memories come to
linger — brightly as the tongues of flame leap
ever higher — and sometimes dimly — as the
shadows move in endless patterns on the wall —
                             sometimes
dying with the scattered embers —
                         sometimes
glowing — as the heart remembers —
                         —
                           —
                               —

—
—
—

do you not know —

                        that our lives — both
yours and mine — are woven into one by
countless fragile threads —

                        of different col-
ored dreams —

      and some

           are of the flames
      and some

           are of the ashes —

beside this murky pond —
        I saw
        the Alchemist at work —

drawing a slender green shoot upward from the muddied waters — lifting it ever gently toward the golden sunlight —

and I stood enraptured as the glossy leaves unfolded — to cradle a fragile blossom of incomparable beauty and flawless perfection —

and as the fragrance filled the summer day —

I wondered at the ease with which the Creator transmuted foul mud and ugliness and decay — into shimmering radiance and rare perfume —

and then — in a moment of awareness I knew — that a pond lily too receives its precious gift of life —

from the gentle hands of the great Alchemist —

the rain —
            that brings new life to the
            thirsting earth —
may also —
            wash the cobwebs from the soul —

for it comes from the sky to bless the earth —
and all who live upon it —
                         falling   with   gentle
sounds upon the new-born leaves —
                                   drumming
with monotonous precision upon the parched
fields of summer —
                         sweeping relentlessly across
the resting earth to mute the autumn glory —
                                        and
always washing man's debris from sky and land
— and ever bringing the gift of life —

                                   —

                                      —

                                         —

—
—
—

that man might live amid the beauty of his
world — as it was surely meant to be —
                                        is it
yet too late to lift our eyes toward the
heavens —
        that the falling rain may also
wash the cobwebs
                from the soul —

mere words

      are so

            inadequate —

to tell you —
            of the lonely green of winter's
early sunsets — that often clutch the heart with
chilling fingers —
            or to describe —
                        the liquid gold
of cowslips against the dark spring waters —
                                    or to
share with you —
            the delicate blue of gentians
beside a mirrored lake —
                        mere words — are but
echoes in the sheltered forest — where only the
call of a distant crow drifts upon the summer
air — and the muted whisper of falling hemlock
needles — speak more of destiny than the printed
page —
            words — words are such —
                  fleeting —
                  empty things —

live slowly —
     through each
     fleeting day —
          remembering —
          always remembering —

that a life is but a footstep on the journey
toward perfection —
                    each day a tiny speck upon
the vastness of eternity —
                    each hour a grain of
sand beneath our faltering feet —
                              for time is of
man's own dreaming —
                    and if in some anguished
moment — the shadow of a cloud lies heavy on
your heart —

—

—

—

look quietly at the image of perfection in
the snowflake that has fallen on your
sleeve —
  or hold this bud of laurel in the
shelter of your hand —
    and if doubt still
lingers —
  listen to a breaking wave spend
itself upon the shore —
    and know that in the
precise wisdom of the infinite —
 another wave
   will come
     to take its place —

beauty takes the form of common things —
    a falling tear —
      a budding rose —
        a graceful gull on silver wings —